Gifts of the Seasons, Autumn and Winter

Gifts of the Seasons, Autumn and Winter

Poems by

Suzanne Cottrell

Cover design by Shay Culligan

ISBN: 978-1-952326-14-1

Kelsay Books
502 South 1040 East, A-119
American Fork, Utah, 84003

For my mom, Patricia Jennings Murray, whose love of the literary, visual, and performing arts is contagious.

For my stepmom, Katie Bush Berry, who shares her love of flowers, floral arrangements, and cats.

For my mother-in-law, Berenice Satterwhite Cottrell, who enjoyed reading and going on picnics.

Acknowledgments

Special thanks to my family, especially my loving husband Bob and daughter Sara, for their ideas, editing, encouragement, and support.

My appreciation goes to the Granville County Senior Center Writers' Group for critiquing my poetry and inspiring me to keep writing.

My thanks to the following publications and their editors for accepting my work.

Cagibi Literary: "Wintry Liberation"
Fall Avocet: "A Sensory Awakening"
Haiku Journal: "Blazing scarlet sun," "Snow covered pansies,"
   "Suspended halo"
NatureWriting: "More Snow," "Slow Melt," "Wintry S'mores"
Plum Tree Tavern: "Wintry Treats"
Poetry in Plain Sight: "Autumn Acrobats," "Murmuration"
Poetry Quarterly: "Beacon," "Dancing Leaves," "On Ice,"
   "Wintry Banquet"
The Pangolin Review: "Escape"
The Weekly Avocet: "Hibernation," "Nature Calls," "Night Flash,"
   "Nightly woods' silence," "Rambunctious squirrels,"
   "Scampering chipmunk," "Snowfall Artistry," "Swaying tree
   tops"
Three Line Poetry: "Pristine snowfall blankets"
Winter Avocet: "Rhythmic Journey," "The Perfect Snowball,"
   "Wintry Silhouettes, "Beacon"

Contents

A Sensory Awakening

Farewell summer, welcome autumn
Arousing my senses

A collage of vibrant hues: crimson, butterscotch, rust, and
mahogany
Fallen leaves strewn across the lawn awaiting rakes
The subtle, fading colors of wilting flowers
Brilliant emerald and jade evergreens
Dark brown locust pods, ambrosia for the deer
Fields of robust orange to pale white, deep-ribbed pumpkins
Trees heavy laden with juicy apples
Daylight hours gradually diminishing

Canada Geese honking, announcing their arrival
Wind gusts rustling leaves
Chattering squirrels foraging for nuts
Acorns crunching beneath my feet
Crickets singing slower melodies
As the temperature drops
Cozy fires crackling
Knitting needles clicking

A menu of olfactory contrasts
Musty, decaying vegetation
Fresh, ripened fruit
Smokey wood burning
Crisp, clean air
Woolens from the cedar chest
Inviting spices of cinnamon, nutmeg, and cloves

A pleasing palate of pungent spices
Homemade hearty soups
First frost greens of kale and collards
Thick, sweet maple syrup
Caramel coated apples sticking in my teeth
Gingerbread, molasses cookies, apple pie, and apple butter
Tantalizing my taste buds

Sticky tree sap
Prickly hay bales and pine needles
Velvety whitetail deer antlers
Blustery breezes
Bounding into a pile of dry, brittle leaves
My hands cupped around a mug of steaming cider

Captivated by the awakening of my autumn senses,
Rejoicing in a bountiful harvest.

Night Flash

Driving over Falls Lake Bridge
One balmy September night
Contemplating the day's events
Attempting to wind down
From a hectic day at work
Shadows of clouds
Chasing the moonlight
Alone, comforted by the calmness
Then a spontaneous burst
Of brilliant aquamarine light
Against the slate night sky
Unlike the meteors seen before,
White blazes across the night sky,
Diving toward the horizon
This meteor, a celestial grenade,
Must have been of unusual size and speed
An instantaneous, spectacular vision
A momentary distraction
To my serene drive home

Nature Calls

Chilled air on an October afternoon.
Draped in a wool, Tartan shawl,
Sitting in my oak rocking chair
On our rustic, wide, front porch,
Gently rocking to my own cadence,
Attuned to nature's varying rhythms.

Recognizing the familiar call
Of a flaming, red cardinal
Seeming to say, "Pretty, pretty, pretty."
The sporadic chattering of gray squirrels
As they protect their gathered seeds.

In the background is the constant buzzing, "REE..."
Of the male cicadas serenading.
The females are content to listen, like me.
Then the emphatic utterance,
The bass bellow of a bull frog.
Countered by the treble chirps of crickets.

A flock of migrating Canada Geese
In their V-formation overhead
Honking throughout their synchronized flight.
The interrupting, hoarse caw of crows
Ravaging the corn field remnants
In my view across the gravel road.

Detached from the city's cacophony,
Calm and relaxed, I listen to nature's calls.
As a crisp breeze whistles through the trees
And tired leaves flutter to the ground
My brief respite from household chores is waning.

Lake Reflections

While we hiked the two and a half mile trail around scenic Price
　　Lake
On a brisk October afternoon we spotted the emerald head of a
　　Mallard drake

Stepped over a protruding Shagbark Hickory root
Glimpsed a scurrying chipmunk with its harvested loot

Paused to peer over a weathered bridge's wooden rails
At brown trout minnows pooled in the shallows and snails

The trickling mountain water of Cold Prong Stream
Beavers challenged its flow with their dam upstream

Paused to examine chiseled markings on a yellow birch stump
A steeper trail grade slowed our pace, required our arms to pump

Strolled along the boardwalk laid over marshy terrain
Sunlight streamed through evergreens suffering from acid rain

Recognized the need to become a partner for a remedy
To save the beauty of the lake and woods in jeopardy

Rounded the far end of the placid, mountain lake
A mound of boulders, remnants of a shifting plate

Listened to the gentle, lapping waves along the stony shoreline
A grey heron at water's edge sought a fish on which to dine

Scaled up granite slabs to our favorite vantage rock
We perched a safe distance from the edge while we took stock

Of nature's wonders, the grandeur of Grandfather Mountain set the
    stage
Canada Geese honked overhead while we admired the beautiful
    mirror image

Of a collage of autumn foliage, mountain tops, billowing clouds
Reflected in the lake's clear, glassy surface far from urban crowds

A fish bit at the surface; concentric circles rippled
White pines sheltered us as rain drizzled

We followed the rolling, uneven wooded path
Hastened steps to avoid the rainstorm's wrath

As the trail wound its way through thick rhododendron and fern
An obstacle course of vegetation forced us to duck and turn

Reached the walkway across the dam by the Blue Ridge Parkway
The rain gradually subsided; a brilliant rainbow brightened this day

We looped through the campground; our hike neared its end
A memorable experience with stories to share, a trail to recommend

Murmuration

Boisterous chatter
Black feathered birds
Perched on oak and elm branches
Pointing my finger, connecting the dots
Of the enormous starling flock
Spontaneously triggered
Skilled acrobatic flight
Orchestrated as a
Massive inky cloud
Swerving and maneuvering
Resembling a meandering river
Of murky water
Then settling in
Before instantaneous flight

Autumn Short Poems

Scampering chipmunk
Chubby cheeks stuffed with acorns
Fall preparation

Old branches creak
Leaves rustle in the fierce wind
Tumble to the ground

Rambunctious squirrels
Spiraling up an oak tree
Chasing, chattering

Swaying tree tops
Windy Argentine Tango
Limbs leaning, bending

Acorn castanets
Dry, crunching leaves under foot
Autumn percussion
Chilled wind swishes through branches
Groaning, cracking, snapping drums

Fall cyclone of leaves
Erratic distribution
Awaiting raking
Piling leaves into high mounds
Children eager to jump in

Nightly woods' silence
Great Horned Owl's interruptions
Deep, serial hoots

Woodland Discoveries

Musty, loamy smell saturates the woods.
Damp leaves, moss cushion my steps.
Sunlight streams through partially bare branches.
Water droplets, fluid prisms, dangle
from remaining leaf tips. Plop upon my head.
I run my fingertips over tree bark scratches,
scars left by a porcupine.

Water gurgles in a creek,
overflows its banks from recent rains.
I take deliberate steps across
smooth, slick stones, logs
felled by industrious beavers.
I suspect a dam lies upstream.

I turn over a rotting log, hop back
as a spotted salamander scurries
under decomposing leaves,
wood frog clucks displeasure
at being disturbed.
I roll the log back into the mud.

Serrated holly fern leaves border my trail.
I spot burnished cambium where
whitetail bucks rubbed off antler velvet.
Giant, yellow Hyssop curtsy in the breeze.
Squish, dark purple chokeberries
scattered by birds stain my boot soles.

I continue my hike over rolling terrain.
Striking blue asters cluster at base of a hickory tree.
Tiger swallowtail butterfly
flits from blossom to blossom.
I pause, drink some water, reflect on
my discoveries, woods' serene beauty.

Dancing Leaves

Audience sits on front porch rockers.
Yard transforms into elegant ballroom.
Sunlight casts spotlight on performers.
Wildlife orchestra warms up.
Red-headed woodpecker taps out the beat.
Song sparrows chirp lively rhythms.
Wind choreographs a fusion dance
of fallen multi-colored, shaped leaves.
They glide, rise and fall, zig zag
across the dance floor in a Quick Step.
Then in a loose embrace, leaves
promenade, swivel, and execute
leg wraps around fallen twigs as
they perform a torrid Tango.
Wind whistles and roars approval.
Onlookers applaud.

Spiritual Awakening

Hoarfrost glazes jade grass blades.
White yard glistens this December morning.
Dense, smoky fog settles as clouds hug the ground.
Brisk breeze kisses rosy cheeks.
A white orb peeks through at the horizon.
Sun renders an eerie illumination.

Soul detaches from physical body,
Hang glides effortlessly above the cloaked terrain.
A river of emotions floods heightened consciousness.
Visual lenses adjust to the changing light.
Vivid images reveal miniscule surface details.

Like a rock climber resting on a narrow ledge
Examines panoramic view of life,
Places events in perspective.
Soft whisper instills, "It's not your time."
Fear of future no longer consumes.

Magnifying white light releases its gravitational pull.
Peace and love envelop spiritual essence.
Mind grapples with soul's re-entry into aging body,
Hesitating to forgo the transcendental experience.

As the fog lifts, sunlight transitions to golden mustard.
Frozen dew melts, creates water droplet prisms.
Winding asphalt absorbs wave lengths of light, radiates warmth,
Guides feet along earthly path.
Life's purpose redefined.

Beacon

January evening walk with Bear,
our Shepherd-Labrador mix,
full moon lights our path.

Arctic gusts shove us along,
our strides keep up with
lengthening shadows.

Our breaths form clouds.
Bundled up in heavy coats,
exposed skin stings.

Shivering branches wave,
wind whistles, a signal
that hurries us on our walk.

Frosted sweet gum leaves, scattered
starfish glisten. Seed balls tumble
like sea urchins in the surf.

I long for barefoot massages
on warm, white, sandy beaches.
Instead, my clunky boots

traverse uneven, frozen
ground. The iced moon serves
as our beacon back home.

Snowfall Artistry

Overnight snowfall settles.
Frost embosses window panes.
Bejeweled flower crystals
sparkle in morning sunlight.

Snowflakes swirl all directions
before they stick, rest, cling.
Powdery robes clothe naked trees.
Layered blankets cover grass, shrubs.

Wind like an artist's knife
shapes textured snow drifts.
Perpetual cycle as
heavy snow accumulates.

Squirrel grasping a walnut
pops up through snow bank,
climbs atop wooden fence post,
gnaws on winter snack.

Escape

Chilled sunrise,
smoky mist rises
off vast snow fields

Cloaks mystical castle
with glistening silver spires,
ice glazed branches tower

Within salt water taffy sky,
bands of seafoam green,
heather lilac, cotton candy pink

Pastel colors fade into
creamy pastures as a magical
beast, rare albino buck, leaps,

eludes archers' arrows, sun rays
stream, fog dissipates,
frosted illusion retreats.

Winter Short Poems

Lace, crystal doilies
Swirl softly toward the ground
Catch them with your tongue

Pristine snowfall blankets the land.
Bare branches wear fluffy, white robes.
A red cardinal perches in an evergreen.

Snow-covered pansies
Insulated from harsh cold
Fitly re-emerge

Suspended halo
Ice crystals caress the moon
Frigid, hushed moon dogs

Blazing scarlet sun
sinks behind brush fire of clouds
consumes winter day

Winter's Deception

Bundled up
   Down-filled jacket
      Flannel-lined jeans
        Alpaca socks
           Insulated boots
              Woolen scarf, cap
                Knitted mittens

Venture outside
For a wintry hike

Contrasting beauty
   Evergreen branches
      Plump crimson berries
        Icy blue crystals
          Pristine snow
             Deciduous taupe limbs
             Saffron grasses

Blast of arctic air
Slaps face
Stings rosy cheeks
Breath vapor condenses
Forming miniature clouds
Steps upon frozen terrain
Jar feet, legs
Muscles tense
Stationary shudder
Glance disbelieving
Thermometer reads two degrees
Winter's sunshine deceives

Temporary Traces

Overnight anticipation,
I awaken to a
monochromatic canvas.
Fresh snow reveals
trails of criss-crossing
wildlife steps.
I behold deer hooves,
rabbit tracks, bird footprints.
Later more snowfall
erases my discoveries, creates
new monochromatic canvas,
for zig zagging patterns.

Wintry Banquet

Late one frigid January afternoon,
Mother Nature set our house and yard
like a holiday banquet.

Lace tablecloth and
placemats of intricate
snowflakes welcomed us.

Animal tracks in the snow
like delicate accents on
ivory China plates.

We traced our fingers on the
etched, alabaster window panes,
nature's Waterford crystal.

Songbirds' punch bowl,
a frozen bird bath,
sparkled in the sunlight.

Garden of icy glazed
vegetables--Brussel sprouts,
cabbage, kale, asparagus.

Melting icicles dangled from our roof,
drizzles of sugary icing on
a warmed spice cake.

Invitation accepted,
we donned our winter coats
eager to partake in her
wintry banquet.

Wintry Treats

Birds flit, flutter
Frenzy at bird feeder
Chickadee alights on limb
Waiting its turn
Loose seeds sprinkle
Powdery snow below
Sparrows hop and peck
Exposing stirred up dirt
Unheated bird bath becomes
Miniature ice rink
Doves sip through crack
Thrushes feast on clusters
Of violet Beautyberries
Persistent gray squirrel
Excavates black walnut
Clasps hidden treasure
Gnaws and chews
Enjoying wintry treats

Wintry S'Mores

Ice flecks sparkle in snow covered yard
Decorated by animal tracks,
Protruding wild grasses, shifting shadows

Half hidden nuts resemble chocolate chips
Marshmallow, snowcapped fence posts
Protrude from graham cracker soil
Savor winter's dessert

More Snow

Overcast January morning
Flurries at dawn
Anticipated forecast
One to two inches

Driveway, sidewalk covered
Shoveled off porch and steps
Footprints quickly vanished
Three to four inches

Snowfall intensified
Like a down feather pillow fight
Limited visibility
Five to six inches

Laden branches bent
Under the weight
Tree limbs moaned
Seven to eight inches

Fallen tree limbs
Power outages
Temperatures plummeted
Nine to ten inches

Snow accumulated
Exceeded expectations
Sculpted landscape,
Frozen beauty

Rhythmic Journey

Compacted, snow-covered trails,
woods in hushed stillness
until my cross country skis chatter,
scritch, scratch, scritch, scratch,
scrape across snow crystals,
sugary snow sparkles.

Opposing arms and legs swing
like pendulums, rhythmically I
glide over rolling terrain,
ski within firm, parallel grooves.
Rabbit tracks crisscross the
adjacent cream-colored snow.

Sunlight trickles through evergreens
veiled in clouds of chilled fog.
Fragrant pine scent diffuses the forest.
Sun-cupped snow, melted pockets,
expose protruding blades of grass.

Swish, swish, swish
My powerful, alternating strides
like spreading cream cheese on a toasted bagel.
Lyrical locomotion invigorates me.
My heart beats quicken as I ascend each rise.
Snow softens the rapping of a distant woodpecker.

Hands of the wind shape
slabs of snow into masterful sculptures.
Swirls of ivory dust resemble
ballerina's pirouettes a top
my childhood music box playing
Tchaikovsky's "Swan Lake."

Moved by the picturesque scenery
captured in a Norman Rockwell painting,
I ski on, bathed in the placid
beauty of the wintry woods.

The Perfect Snowball

The long awaited arrival of
a pristine, wet snow
warmed by the winter's sun

Gloved hands readied
to make frozen projectiles
A snowball formed with
    clean snow- no evidence of dirt or tinges of yellow
        pure snow- no ice shards or bits of gravel
            pliable snow- no rigidity or crumbling

Hands cupped held scoops of snow
gently caressed, molded, rotated
until the snowball resisted pressure
firmly packed, smoothed over rough edges
A perfectly, chilled, seamless baseball

Arm cocked back, then forward motion
fingers released grip, snowball launched
stayed intact, broke upon impact
dusted the intended target
The Perfect Snowball!

Wintry Silhouettes

January Saturday night
Crisp, biting air
Frozen farm pond
Strategically placed bonfire
Snap, pop, crackle, hiss
Warm, amber glow
Smoke wafted, curled
Toward bare treetops

Seated on oak log
Laced up ice skates
Stepped deliberately
Onto bluish-gray ice
With a wide, bristled brush
Swept snow from pond surface
Stiff, leaning, wobbling postures
Squealing, human bumper cars

Grabbed, clinged,
Pulled around the ice
Spontaneous giggling
Skate blades' irregular scrollings
Rosy cheeks, puffs of breath vapor

Frosted eye lashes glistened
Sweeping arms, longer strides
Glided then bobbled
Over ice ridges, swoosh,
Clink, etching figure-eights

On Ice

Dappled clouds cloak the sun
January sunrise, head out
Dressed in thermal layers
Insulated, waterproof boots
Breath vapor crystalizes

Winds bluster
Ice overtakes Lake Champlain
Walleye, bass, Northern pike glide
Underneath glacial, blue ice
Solid along forested shoreline

Wary anglers take deliberate steps
Like walking on tightropes
Looking for dips, bubbles
Listening for crackles, pops
Alert to ice surface changes

Drag loaded sleds across ice field
Select promising spots for ice fishing
Handheld augers drill through
Ice, 1, 2, 3, 4 inches deep
Swiss cheese ice holes dot the lake

Chisels, widening holes
Configure jigging rods, tip ups
Frigid air challenges ungloved fingers
Bait lines with minnows
Sit on overturned buckets

Re-gloved hands jerk rods up and down
Keeping pace with heart beats
Waiting, waiting, waiting
Common Redpolls swirl overhead
Sharp, staccato calls pierce

Silence, solitude among ice fishermen
Strike, red flag releases
Signals first catch of the day
Fish twists, tugs to break lose
Angler's adrenalin surges, muscles tighten

Firm, steady hold; reels it in
Fish head breaks water's surface
Pulls up walleye, smack onto the ice
Flips, flops, olive scales shimmer
Measures 26 inches, a keeper

Clears icy hole by
Skimming slush away
Resets tip up, rebaits line
Wet, numb fingers grasp thermos
Hot chocolate melts coldness

More waiting, waiting
Stillness consumes frozen landscape
Red flags periodically pop up
Like prairie dog heads
A prosperous day on ice

Hibernation

Stretching bare deciduous branches
Quivering in the Arctic wind
Casting shadows as skeletal lines

Bathing in the winter sun
Purple, yellow, and red pansies
Markings creating their faces

Blanketing snow overnight
Covering the frozen ground
Crisscrossing wild, rabbit tracks

Bundling up and pulling on boots
Plodding and plowing through snow drifts
Catching tiny snowflakes on my tongue

Contrasting a red cardinal
Against the evergreens and snow
Searching for mulberries and seeds

Filling up the birdfeeder
With their favorite sunflower seeds
Waiting for birds to perch and snack

Sledding, ice skating, and snow ball fights
Making snow angels and eating snow cream
Shivering with a rosy nose and cheeks, then

Hibernating through the bitter cold
Curling up with an engaging book
Sipping a cup of soothing, hot chocolate, aaaaaaah!

Wintry Liberation

Sheltered from
Blustery winds
Whiteout conditions
Siberian wind chill

Enveloped by a
Crackling fire's warmth
Settled comfortably
Eyes closed
Breathing naturally

In pursuit of
Mindful fitness
Freezing emotions to
Preserve cherished memories
Fluttering within a snow globe

Encouraging worldly thoughts
To lie dormant or
Drift through
Emptying any trash
Cleansing and liberating as the frigid air

Slow Melt

Winter sun radiates warmth
Clumps of snow
Nestled in tree forks till
Like a falling scoop
Of ice cream, plop
Ivory, fairy dust drifts

Shrinking blanket on
Decaying log in slumber
Snow draped Azalea bushes
Doff ermine's fur coat

Jolly snowman
Gradually leans
Altered features
Now undistinguishable

Water droplets trickle
Down translucent stalactites
Drips splash, pitting
Snow underneath

Slabs of snow crack
Sliding off house roofs
Avalanche cascades
Creating mounds below

Silence of powdery snow
Transforms into slush
Freezes overnight
Morning footsteps
Crunch on icy crust
Boots breaking through

Daily temperatures warm
Melting snow and ice
Inch by inch
Day after day
Till only shimmering
Pools remain

About the Author

Suzanne Cottrell lives with her husband and three rescued dogs in rural Piedmont North Carolina. An outdoor enthusiast and retired teacher, she enjoys reading, writing, knitting, hiking, Pilates, and yoga. She loves nature's sensory stimuli and experimenting with poetry. Her poems have appeared in numerous journals and anthologies including the *Best Emerging Poets Series*, *Avocet, Plum Tree Tavern, Poetry Quarterly, Burningword Journal,* and *The Pangolin Review.* She was the recipient of 2017 Rebecca Lard Poetry Award, Prolific Press.

https://suzanneswords.com

www.ingramcontent.com/pod-product-compliance
Lightning Source LLC
Chambersburg PA
CBHW031154090426
42738CB00008B/1332